THE ANSWER Workbook

Joseph Brice

Dedication

To the readers of "The Answer" workbook,

This workbook is dedicated to you, the seekers of truth, the dreamers of dreams, and the faithful followers on the path to spiritual enlightenment. Your courage to ask questions, your dedication to growth, and your unwavering faith in the journey set you apart as beacons of hope and inspiration.

May this workbook serve as a guiding light, helping you navigate life's challenges with grace and wisdom. May it empower you to discover the answers that lie within, and may it strengthen your relationship with God, enriching your life with purpose, peace, and profound joy.

To all who open these pages with an open heart and mind, know that you are cherished and supported. Your journey is a testament to the enduring power of faith and the boundless possibilities that lie ahead.

Thank you for allowing "The Answer" to be a part of your spiritual journey. May you find clarity, comfort, and divine guidance in every word and exercise.

With deep gratitude and blessings,

Joseph Brice

Preface

Welcome to "The Answer Workbook," a companion guide designed to deepen your engagement with the themes and lessons of Joseph Brice's thought-provoking book, *The Answer: Not What I Imagined*. This workbook aims to transform the insights from the book into practical, actionable steps that can enrich your spiritual journey and personal growth.

"The Answer: Not What I Imagined" by Joseph Brice dives deep into the transformative power of faith-filled speech and the significant role our words play in shaping our reality and fulfilling our divine purpose.

"Faith to Speak" is a profound exploration of how the words we choose can either build up or tear down, not just in our lives, but in the lives of those around us. The Bible is replete with teachings on the power of the tongue, emphasizing that life and death are indeed in the power of our words. Jesus Himself demonstrated the profound impact of speaking with faith, whether calming a storm, healing the sick, or raising the dead.

In this book, we will unpack the biblical principles that underscore the importance of aligning our speech with our faith. We will examine the stories of individuals who harnessed the power of their words to effect change and bring about God's promises. One such example is the story of the centurion, whose faith in Jesus' spoken word led to the miraculous healing of his servant.

The workbook for is designed to help you harness the power of your own words through practical exercises, reflective questions, and thought-provoking discussions. These activities are crafted to encourage you to examine the language you use daily and to consciously choose words that reflect your faith and trust in God's promises.

Through this book, you will be challenged to speak with intentionality and conviction, understanding that your words can influence outcomes and manifest the divine will in your life. As you engage with the content, you will learn to replace negative speech patterns with declarations of faith, hope, and love.

Embrace this journey with a heart ready to be transformed. By developing the faith to speak life and truth into your circumstances, you can unlock the power of God's word in your own life. Let your speech become a testament to your faith, and witness the remarkable changes that follow.

As you work through the exercises and reflections in this workbook, may you find your voice strengthened and your faith emboldened. May your words become a powerful force for good, aligning with the divine purpose God has set for you.

In *The Answer: Not What I Imagined*, Joseph explores profound concepts surrounding faith, purpose, and divine timing. Each chapter presents a unique perspective on how we can discover and embrace our true answers amidst the complexities and challenges of life. This workbook extends these ideas, offering you a structured approach to reflect, apply, and integrate the book's teachings into your daily life.

Why a Workbook?

While reading the book provides valuable insights and inspiration, a workbook allows you to engage with these ideas more deeply. Through exercises, reflections, and assignments, you can explore how the principles discussed in the book relate to your own experiences. This interactive approach helps bridge the gap between understanding and action, guiding you in applying the lessons learned to real-life situations.

What to Expect

The workbook is divided into sections that correspond with the chapters of *The Answer: Not What I Imagined*. Each chapter in this workbook begins with an introduction that recaps the key themes and provides context for the exercises that follow. You'll find prompts designed to encourage introspection, practical activities to apply the teachings, and spaces for personal notes and reflections.

How to Use This Workbook

1. **Read and Reflect:** Start by reading the corresponding chapter from the book. Take time to ponder the concepts and how they resonate with your own life.

2. **Engage with the Exercises:** Use the exercises in the workbook to explore these ideas further. Write down your thoughts, answers, and reflections. The more engaged you are, the more you'll gain from this experience.

3. **Apply the Insights:** Consider how the insights from each chapter can be applied to your personal circumstances. Reflect on how they might influence your decisions, actions, and interactions with others.

4. **Review and Reflect:** Periodically review your responses and reflections. This ongoing process will help solidify your understanding and track your growth over time.

A Journey of Transformation

The purpose of this workbook is not just to provide answers, but to facilitate a journey of transformation. As you work through the exercises and apply the principles discussed, you'll find that your perspective on challenges and opportunities evolves. This process will enable you to align more closely with your true purpose and embrace the answers that God has for you.

Thank you for embarking on this journey with *The Answer Workbook*. May it serve as a guide and a companion as you explore the depths of faith, purpose, and divine timing in your life.

Be cautious not to dismiss your answered prayer simply because it doesn't align with your expectations. This is a common pitfall that many people fall into, as The Religious Leaders known as The Pharisees miss out on recognizing Jesus because He didn't fit their preconceived image of a messiah. Similarly, we might overlook our blessings if we are too fixated on what the answer should look like.

Remember, the part we can do, we should do; the things far beyond our reach are the part we give to God.

Today, we face many challenges, and people want answers. When we pray, we should strive to have faith in God, knowing that **Jesus is The Answer!**

Contents

Take Heed

Take Heed to your calling and be mindful of the subtle influences and distractions that can lead us away from our true purpose and divine calling.

Jesus frequently admonished His followers to be watchful and alert. This book explores His teachings on the necessity of spiritual discernment and the dangers of complacency. By examining biblical examples and contemporary applications, we learn how to guard our hearts and minds against the pitfalls that threaten our spiritual growth.

The story of Judas Iscariot provides a stark illustration of the consequences of failing to heed Jesus' warnings. Despite being one of the twelve disciples, Judas allowed greed and disillusionment to corrupt his heart, leading to his betrayal of Jesus. This tragic account serves as a powerful reminder that even those closest to the truth can falter if they do not remain vigilant.

In this workbook, you will find reflective questions, practical exercises, quizzes, and discussion prompts designed to help you internalize the lessons of each Chapter. These activities will encourage you to assess your own spiritual state, identify areas where you need to be more watchful, and develop strategies to strengthen your faith and commitment.

Our goal is to equip you with the tools to stay alert and steadfast in your walk with God. By taking heed of Jesus' teachings and the examples set forth in the Bible, you can avoid the snares of the enemy and remain true to your divine calling.

Approach this book with an open mind and a willing spirit, ready to learn and grow. As you engage with the content, may you develop a heightened sense of spiritual awareness and a deeper commitment to living a life that honors God. Through vigilance and faithfulness, you can navigate the challenges of this world and stay on the path to your ultimate purpose.

"Always pray and watch as well as pray."

"Take heed to yourselves: if your brother trespass against you, rebuke him, and if he repent, forgive him." Luke 17: 3.

"Take heed to yourselves, that your heart be not deceived, and turnaway from God to serve other gods , and worship them." Deuteronomy 23:12

"Take heed, brethren, lest there be in any of you an evil heart of unbelief, in departing from the living God." Hebrews 3:12

Take heed, if you think you are standing firm, be careful that you don't fall!" 1 Corinthians 10:12.

Encouragement for Leaders

Sometimes, as leaders, you may find yourself in a position where it feels like there is no one you can confide in. The weight of responsibility can be overwhelming, and the isolation that often accompanies leadership can leave you feeling alone and unsupported. However, before you consider giving up, take a moment to reflect on the value of what you have and who you are to God.

As a leader, you possess unique qualities and strengths that have been entrusted to you for a purpose. Your role is not just a position of authority but a calling that carries profound significance. You are a beacon of hope, a source of guidance, and an instrument of positive change in the lives of those you lead. The impact you have on others is immeasurable, and your dedication to your mission is a testament to your resilience and commitment.

In times of doubt and solitude, remember that you are not truly alone. God, who has called you to this path, is always with you. He sees your struggles, understands your challenges, and offers His unwavering support and love. Your relationship with God is a sanctuary where you can find solace, wisdom, and strength. He is your confidant, your refuge, and your source of inspiration.

Consider the value of what you have achieved and the lives you have touched. Your leadership has brought hope to the hopeless, direction to the lost, and encouragement to the weary. The seeds of kindness, wisdom, and guidance you have sown will continue to grow and flourish, even in ways you may not immediately see.

Reflect on who you are to God. You are His beloved child, chosen and cherished. Your worth is not determined by the challenges you face or the burdens you carry but by the infinite love and grace of your Creator. He has equipped you with the talents and abilities needed to fulfill your purpose, and He believes in your potential even when you may doubt it yourself.

Before you consider throwing it all away, take a step back and see the bigger picture. Your journey as a leader is part of a greater plan, one that is woven with divine intention and purpose. Trust that God has a purpose for every season of your life, including the difficult ones. Your perseverance and faith in the face of adversity are not only a testament to your strength but also a beacon of hope for others.

Lean into your faith, seek God's guidance, and allow His presence to renew your spirit. Surround yourself with those who uplift and encourage you, and don't hesitate to reach out for support when needed. Remember, even leaders need a helping hand and a listening ear.

Ultimately, your value as a leader and as a child of God is immeasurable. Embrace the journey, cherish the lessons learned, and continue to lead with compassion, integrity, and faith. The world needs your light, your wisdom, and your unwavering commitment to making a difference. You are not alone, and your efforts are not in vain.

"May God bless you and keep you: The Lord make his face shine upon you, and be gracious to you:The Lord lift up his face upon you, and give you peace." Number 6 :24-26.

Workbook Chapter One:

The Miracle

Welcome to the workbook for Chapter 1, "The Miracle," from "The Answer: Not What I Imagined" by Joseph Brice. This chapter sets the foundation for understanding how miracles are not just extraordinary events but divine interventions that reveal God's power and purpose in our lives.

In "The Miracle," we delve into the essence of miracles and their significance in the biblical narrative and our personal faith journeys. Miracles are often seen as the tangible evidence of God's presence and activity in the world, transcending natural laws and expectations. From the parting of the Red Sea to the resurrection of Jesus Christ, the Bible is filled with accounts of miraculous events that demonstrate God's sovereignty and love for His people.

This chapter invites you to explore how miracles can manifest in your own life and encourages you to recognize and celebrate the miracles that often go unnoticed. By examining the stories of biblical figures who experienced God's miraculous interventions, you will gain insight into how faith, obedience, and a receptive heart are crucial in positioning ourselves to receive and witness miracles.

The workbook for Chapter 1 is designed to help you deepen your understanding of miracles through practical exercises, reflective questions, and engaging activities. These elements aim to help you identify the miracles in your life, understand the conditions that facilitate their occurrence, and strengthen your faith in God's ability to work wonders in your circumstances.

As you engage with this chapter, you will be encouraged to:

- Reflect on personal experiences where you have witnessed or experienced a miracle.
- Examine biblical accounts of miracles to understand the principles that underlie these divine interventions.
- Develop a mindset that is open to recognizing and expecting miracles in your daily life.
- Strengthen your faith and trust in God's power to perform miracles, no matter how challenging your situation may seem.

By the end of this chapter, you will have a renewed perspective on the role of miracles in your life and be equipped with practical tools to cultivate a faith that is expectant and receptive to God's miraculous power.

Embrace this journey with an open heart and a spirit of anticipation. As you work through the exercises and reflections, may you find your faith strengthened and your eyes opened to the miraculous possibilities that God has in store for you. Let this chapter be a testament to the boundless power of God and His unwavering desire to intervene in your life in miraculous ways.

Questions for Reflection

1   Miraculous Existence

- Reflect on your birth and early childhood. What specific events or circumstances make you consider your existence a miracle?
- How do you see the hand of God or a higher power in your creation and life journey so far?

2   Unique Purpose

- o In what ways do you believe you are a unique creation designed for a specific purpose?
- o How can you embrace and celebrate your uniqueness in your daily life?

3 Faith and Intervention

- o Recall a time when you faced a significant challenge. How did divine intervention or faith play a role in overcoming it?
- o How can the memory of past interventions help you face current or future challenges?

4 Being a Miracle to Others

- o Describe a time when you were able to help someone else in a way that felt miraculous to them.
- o How can you be more aware of opportunities to be a miracle for others in your community?

5 Parent-Child Relationships

- o Reflect on the role your parents or guardians played in your life. How did their actions demonstrate miraculous love and care?
- o How can you support and nurture the next generation in a way that reflects the miracles of life?

Reflection Prompts

1   Gratitude for Life

- Write a letter to yourself expressing gratitude for the miracle of your existence. Highlight specific events that have shaped your life.
- Reflect on a daily basis on the small miracles that occur in your life and note them in a gratitude journal.

2   Self-Worth and Purpose

- Spend time in meditation or prayer, asking for clarity on your unique purpose in life. Write down any insights or revelations you receive.
- Create a vision board that represents your unique gifts and the impact you wish to make in the world.

3   Faith in Action

- Reflect on the story of Moses and his mother. How does their faith and courage inspire you to act in your own life?
- Identify a current challenge you are facing. Write a prayer or affirmation asking for divine intervention and expressing trust in a higher power.

4   Community and Service

- Volunteer for a cause that resonates with you. Reflect on how your actions, no matter how small, can be a miracle for someone else.

- o   Identify a person in your life who may need encouragement or support. Reach out to them and offer your help or a listening ear.

Practice Exercises

1   Gratitude Exercise

- o   Each morning, list three things you are grateful for, focusing on the miraculous aspects of your life. At the end of the week, review your list and reflect on the patterns you see.

2   Acts of Kindness

- o   Perform at least one act of kindness each day for a week. Reflect on how these actions impact others and how they make you feel.

3   Prayer and Meditation

- o   Dedicate 10-15 minutes each day to prayer or meditation, focusing on asking for guidance and recognizing the miracles in your life. Journal any thoughts or feelings that arise.

4   Letter to Your Future Self

- o   Write a letter to your future self, detailing your hopes, dreams, and the miracles you wish to see unfold in your life. Seal it and set a reminder to read it one year from now.

5   Parental Appreciation

- ○   If possible, interview your parents or guardians about their experiences and challenges during your early years. Reflect on their stories and write a thank-you note expressing your gratitude for their love and sacrifices.

Group Discussion Questions

1   Miracles in Everyday Life

- ○   Share a personal story with the group about a time when you experienced or witnessed a miracle. How did it change your perspective on life?

2   Faith and Challenges

- ○   Discuss the role of faith in overcoming life's challenges. How do stories like those of Moses and Hannah inspire you to maintain faith during difficult times?

3   Being a Miracle for Others

- ○   Brainstorm ways in which you can collectively support and serve your community. How can you create a network of miracles within your group?

4   Parental Influence

- ○   Reflect on the influence of parents or guardians in

shaping who you are today. Share stories of how their actions have been miraculous in your life.

By engaging with these questions, reflections, and exercises, you will deepen your understanding of the miraculous nature of life and your unique role within it. This process will help you appreciate your existence and inspire you to be a source of miracles for others.

Workbook Chapter Two:

When We Pray

Welcome to the workbook for Chapter 2, "When We Pray," from "The Answer: Not What I Imagined" by Joseph Brice. In this chapter, we explore the profound relationship between faith and obedience, emphasizing how faith is essential for truly following God's commands.

Have you ever prayed for something and later realized that the answer you got was not what you expected? It can be confusing, even frustrating. Maybe you rejected the answer and prayed all over again, thinking this couldn't be from God. We must learn to bow to God's will.

When we pray, we often seek solutions to our immediate wants and needs. However, we should not forget that the effects of our prayers can go beyond our own lives. Our prayers may be the answer to someone else's prayers from centuries ago, so we should not underestimate the power of prayer. Its answers can bring hope and inspiration to ourselves and those around us.

The Power of Prayer

Prayer is a powerful tool that connects us with God, allowing us to express our deepest desires, fears, and hopes. One of the most profound examples of the power of prayer is found in the story of Hannah, whose heartfelt prayers were answered in a way that changed her life and the course of history.

The Story of Hannah

Hannah's story is a poignant example of faith, perseverance, and the transformative power of prayer. Hannah was one of two wives of Elkanah. While his other wife, Peninnah, had children, Hannah remained childless. This was a source of deep anguish and sorrow for her, especially because, in her culture, having children was seen as a blessing from God and a sign of a woman's worth.

Year after year, Hannah endured the taunts and provocations of Peninnah, which added to her distress. Despite her husband Elkanah's attempts to comfort her, Hannah's heartache persisted. She longed for a child, and her desire grew stronger each passing year.

Hannah's Earnest Prayer

One year, during their annual pilgrimage to Shiloh to worship and sacrifice to the Lord, Hannah's sorrow reached its peak. In the temple, she poured out her soul to God in a fervent prayer, making a vow:

"O Lord of hosts, if you will indeed look on the affliction of your servant and remember me and not forget your servant, but will give to your servant a son, then I will give him to the Lord all the days of his life, and no razor shall touch his head." (1 Samuel 1:11)

Hannah's prayer was so intense and heartfelt that Eli, the priest, observed her lips moving but heard no sound. He mistakenly thought she was drunk and rebuked her. However, Hannah explained that she was not drunk but was pouring out her soul to the Lord in her distress. Eli, moved by her sincerity, blessed her and prayed that God would grant her request.

God's Answer

God heard Hannah's plea and granted her the desire of her heart. She conceived and bore a son, whom she named Samuel, meaning "heard of God," because she said, "I have asked for him from the Lord." True to her vow, once Samuel was weaned, she brought him to the temple and dedicated him to the Lord's service.

Samuel grew up to become one of the greatest prophets and judges of Israel, leading the nation and anointing its first two kings, Saul and David. Hannah's prayer not only fulfilled her personal longing but also played a pivotal role in the history of Israel.

Prayer is about faith and waiting, patience will be the virtue.

Reflection Questions

1   **Personal Longings**:

- Think about a time when you had a deep desire or longing. How did you express this to God in prayer?
- How did you handle the period of waiting for an answer?

2   **Persistence in Prayer**:

- Reflect on how Hannah persisted in prayer despite her prolonged period of barrenness and the taunting she endured.
- How can you apply Hannah's example of persistence and faith in your own prayer life?

3   **God's Timing and Plan**:

- Consider how God's answer to Hannah's prayer not only fulfilled her desire but also had a greater purpose in His divine plan.
- How can you trust that God's timing and plan for your life are perfect, even when the answers to your prayers seem delayed?

* * *

Practical Exercise: Writing Your Heartfelt Prayer

1   **Identify Your Deepest Longings**:

- Take some time to reflect on your deepest desires and longings. Write them down in a journal, being as honest and detailed as possible.

2   **Pour Out Your Heart to God**:

- Write a heartfelt prayer to God, similar to Hannah's, expressing your deepest emotions and desires. Don't hold back—let God know the full extent of your feelings.

3   **Commit to Persistence**:

- Make a commitment to persist in prayer, regardless of how long it takes to see an answer. Remember that God hears every prayer and will answer in His perfect timing.

Biblical Insights

"Be anxious for nothing, but in everything by prayer and supplication, with thanksgiving, let your requests be made known to God." (Philippians 4:6)

"Ask, and it will be given to you; seek, and you will find; knock, and it will be opened to you." (Matthew 7:7)

Conclusion

Hannah's story is a powerful testament to the effectiveness of earnest and heartfelt prayer. Her unwavering faith and persistence in seeking God's intervention not only brought her personal fulfillment but also contributed significantly to God's broader plan for His people. Like Hannah, we are encouraged to pray earnestly, trust in God's timing, and remain faithful even when the answers are not immediate. Our prayers have the potential to bring about profound changes in our lives and the lives of others, often in ways we cannot foresee.

The workbook for Chapter 2 is designed to help you internalize the lessons from this chapter through reflective questions, practical exercises, and personal applications. These activities aim to strengthen your faith, encourage self-examination, and foster a deeper commitment to prayer.

As you engage with this chapter, you will be encouraged to:

- Reflect on areas in your life where submission to God's will has been challenging.

- Understand the role of prayer in overcoming doubt and fear.

- Explore biblical examples of prayer through faith and draw parallels to your own life.

- Develop strategies to cultivate a lifestyle of prayer

By the end of this chapter, you will have a better understanding of the importance of prayer and be equipped with practical tools to strengthen your prayer life and submitting to God's will.

Approach this workbook with an open heart and a willingness to be transformed. As you work through the exercises and reflections, may you find your prayer life deepened and your resolve to obey God strengthened. Let this be a step toward a life of faithful obedience, trusting in God's perfect plan for your life.

Questions for Reflection

1 Unexpected Answers

- Reflect on a time when you prayed for something and received an unexpected answer. How did you initially react, and how did your understanding of the situation evolve over time?
- What did you learn about God's will and your expectations through that experience?

2 Power of Prayer

- Think about a prayer you made that had a significant impact on someone else's life, even if it wasn't your intention. How did that experience change your perspective on the power of prayer?
- How can you remain mindful of the broader effects your prayers might have on others?

3 Skills and Qualities

- Identify the qualities or skills you possess that could help someone else. How can you use these gifts to support those around you?
- Reflect on a time when you helped someone unexpectedly. How did it feel to be the answer to someone's prayer?

4 Handling "Thorns"

- ○ Like Apostle Paul, reflect on a "thorn" in your life that God has not removed. How has this challenge shaped your faith and character?
- ○ How can you use your struggles to inspire and encourage others?

5   Trusting God's Plan

- ○ Recall a time when God's answer to your prayer was different from what you imagined. How did you learn to trust His plan over your own?
- ○ How can you maintain faith and patience when answers to your prayers are delayed or different from your expectations?

Reflection Prompts

1   Acceptance and Trust

- ○ Write a reflection on the importance of accepting God's will, especially when it differs from your desires. How can you cultivate a heart of trust and submission?
- ○ Reflect on the concept of God's grace being sufficient for you. How can you apply this understanding to your current challenges?

2   Open-Mindedness

- ○ Spend time in prayer or meditation, asking God to help you recognize answers to your prayers that may come in unexpected forms. Write down any insights or realizations.
- ○ Reflect on the story of John the Baptist and the

Pharisees. How can you avoid missing God's answers due to preconceived notions?

3   Gratitude and Respect

- Write a prayer of gratitude, thanking God for the answers to your prayers, even those that were not what you expected. How can you show respect and reverence in your prayer life?
- Reflect on your prayer habits. How can you ensure that your prayers are not just requests but also expressions of love and gratitude?

4   Being an Answer

- Reflect on how you can be more aware of opportunities to be the answer to someone else's prayer. What steps can you take to be more helpful and supportive?
- Write about a recent situation where you felt you were able to help someone. How did that experience impact you and the person you helped?

Practice Exercises

1   Gratitude Exercise

- Each day for a week, write down three things you are grateful for, focusing on how God has answered your prayers in unexpected ways. Reflect on these at the end of the week.

2 Acts of Service

- ○ Identify a skill or quality you possess that can benefit others. Commit to using this gift to help someone in need each day for a week. Reflect on these experiences in a journal.

3 Prayer Journal

- ○ Keep a prayer journal where you record your prayers and the ways they are answered. Reflect on how God's answers align with His greater plan for you and those around you.

4 Daily Prayer Practice

- ○ Dedicate 15 minutes each day to prayer, focusing not just on requests but also on expressing gratitude, seeking God's will, and praying for others. Write about any changes you notice in your relationship with God.

5 Learning from Challenges

- ○ Reflect on a significant challenge in your life that has not been resolved. Write about how you can use this "thorn" to grow spiritually and help others who may be facing similar issues.

Group Discussion Questions

1 Experiences with Unexpected Answers

    ○   Share with the group a time when you received an unexpected answer to your prayer. How did it change your perspective on prayer and God's will?

2   Power of Collective Prayer

    ○   Discuss how collective prayer can have a broader impact. Share examples of how praying for others has brought about unexpected blessings in your own life.

3   Supporting Each Other

    ○   Brainstorm ways your group can support each other and the community, becoming answers to prayers through acts of kindness and service.

4   Overcoming Challenges

    ○   Reflect on how each member has handled significant challenges or "thorns" in their lives. Share stories of how these experiences have helped you grow and inspire others

By engaging with these questions, reflections, and exercises, you will deepen your understanding of prayer's power and its role in aligning with God's will. This process will help you appreciate the unexpected answers and use your experiences to support and inspire others.

Reflection Questions

1   Expectations and Prayer:

- Think about a time when you prayed for something specific. How did you feel when the answer wasn't what you expected?
- How did you handle the situation? Did you pray again or try to understand God's answer?

2   Broader Impact:

- Can you think of a time when your actions, words, or prayers impacted someone else positively? Describe the situation.

Biblical Example: Apostle Paul

The Apostle Paul once disclosed that he prayed to God three times, asking Him to remove the 'thorn in his side.' Paul believed that the removal of the thorn would be the answer to his prayers. However, while waiting, the Lord responded, "My grace is sufficient for you."

- **Personal Reflection**:
    - What are some 'thorns' in your life that you have prayed about?
    - How do you interpret God's response, "My grace is sufficient for you," in your context?

Lessons from John the Baptist and the Pharisees

When John the Baptist came preaching about repentance and baptism, the Pharisees, who knew the prophecy of making the crooked paths straight, rejected him. Even though they witnessed something extraordinary, they could not reconcile John's teachings with their preconceived ideas, causing them to reject his message.

- **Reflection**:
    - How have preconceived notions affected your ability to see God's answers to your prayers?
    - What steps can you take to remain open to God's will, even when it doesn't align with your expectations?

The Importance of Humility in Prayer

It is important to note that even astute men with knowledge of God's Word can miss important details. This emphasizes the significance of always praying and demonstrating humility before God, even when the answer may seem obvious. Seeking God's guidance may be challenging, but it is necessary as it ultimately benefits us and brings glory to God.

- **Self-Examination**:
    - How can you practice humility in your daily prayer life?
    - What are some ways you can seek God's guidance more diligently?

Jesus' Teachings on Prayer

When Jesus was asked to teach us how to pray, He emphasized the importance of showing gratitude and respect to God.

"Our Father in heaven, hallowed be your name. Your kingdom come, your will be done, on earth as it is in heaven. Give us this day our daily bread, and forgive us our debts, as we also have forgiven our debtors. And lead us not into temptation, but deliver us from evil." (Matthew 6:9-13)

- **Application**:
  - How do you incorporate gratitude and respect into your prayers?
  - Reflect on each line of the Lord's Prayer. How can you apply its principles to your daily life?

Trusting God's Plan

Before Jesus went to the cross, he saw a portion of his destiny in a collage of tests and trials in the form of a filled cup. He prayed three times that this cup would pass him, as he did not want to drink from it. God did not answer him. However, in the end, during his third request in prayer, he submitted to God's will and said, "Nevertheless, not my will, but your will be done."

- **Trust and Surrender**:
  - In what areas of your life do you find it challenging to trust God's plan?
  - How can you practice surrendering your will to God in your prayers?

Practical Exercise: Prayer Journal

1 **Daily Prayer Log**:

  - Each day, write down your prayers and any answers or insights you receive.
  - Reflect on how your prayers and God's responses align with His will and your expectations.

2 **Thanksgiving List**:

- o   List five things you are grateful for each day.
- o   Include specific answered prayers and ways you see God working in your life.

Use this chapter as a guide to deepen your prayer life, align with God's will, and become a source of hope and inspiration for others. Remember, your prayers have the power to make a difference not only in your life but also in the lives of those around you.

Closing Prayer

"Dear Lord, I am facing difficult times and challenges that have left me feeling defeated. I know that I am anointed, but in this situation, I feel the anointing alone is not enough to help me overcome my enemies and rise above my circumstances. I humbly ask you to grant me your glory so that I can break free from this grave that I find myself in. You may be struggling with your finances, marriage, divorce, children, relationships overall, or maybe a job or no job at all; it could be your peace or joy. Whatever it is, you need divine intervention to resurrect from this difficult situation. Please grant me your glory, Lord, so that I may glorify your name, Jesus."

Workbook Chapter Three:

In the Waiting

Welcome to the workbook for Chapter 3, "In the Waiting," from "The Answer: Not What I Imagined" by Joseph Brice. This chapter explores one of the most profound and challenging aspects of faith: the waiting period between asking for a divine answer and receiving it.

In our spiritual journeys, waiting for God's response can test our patience and resolve. We often find ourselves caught between hope and despair, wondering why the answers to our prayers seem delayed or uncertain. This chapter focuses on the critical lessons that emerge from waiting and highlights the transformative power of patience.

Chapter 3 delves into the stories of biblical figures like Abraham and Joseph, who faced long periods of waiting and uncertainty. Abraham waited for decades for the fulfillment of God's promise to make him the father of many nations. Despite his and Sarah's advanced age and the many obstacles they faced, their story underscores the importance of maintaining faith and trust in God's timing.

Similarly, Joseph's journey from betrayal and imprisonment to becoming a key figure in Egypt's salvation teaches us about perseverance. His story illustrates how waiting can refine our character and prepare us for greater purposes, even when the process feels unjust or unbearable.

In this workbook, you will:

- **Reflect on the Nature of Waiting:** Understand the spiritual and personal growth that occurs during periods of waiting, and how this time can be used for preparation and transformation.

- **Examine Biblical Examples:** Analyze the stories of Abraham and Joseph to draw lessons on faith, patience, and the importance of remaining steadfast during delays.
- **Identify Your Waiting Periods:** Reflect on areas in your life where you are currently waiting for answers or outcomes, and explore how you can apply the lessons from these biblical narratives to your own experiences.
- **Embrace Patience and Trust:** Engage in exercises that encourage trust in God's timing and develop a deeper understanding of how waiting can lead to significant spiritual and personal breakthroughs.

As you work through this chapter, remember that waiting is not a passive state but an active process of growth and preparation. May the insights and exercises in this workbook help you embrace your own waiting periods with faith and resilience, trusting that God's answers and plans for you are worth the wait.

Reflective Questions

1   **Personal Waiting Periods:**

  - Describe a time in your life when you had to wait for something significant. How did you feel during the waiting period?
  - How did this waiting period impact your faith or belief in God's promises?

2   **Patience and Faith:**

  - What do you think is the most challenging part of waiting on God's promises?
  - How do you keep your faith strong when you feel like giving up?

3   Abraham and Sarah's Story:

- How do Abraham and Sarah's experiences resonate with your personal journey?
- What lessons can you draw from their story about trusting God's timing?

4   Personal Transformation:

- How do you think God might be using your current waiting period to transform you?
- What qualities do you believe you need to develop to be ready for God's promises?

5   Faith in Action:

- What steps can you take to demonstrate your faith while waiting for God's promises?
- How can you remain hopeful and active in your faith during difficult times?

Practice Exercises

1   Journaling Exercise:

- Spend 10-15 minutes each day journaling about your feelings and thoughts during your waiting period. Reflect on how your faith is evolving and any signs of God's work in your life.

2   Prayer Focus:

- Develop a prayer routine that specifically addresses patience and faith. Ask God for strength to endure the waiting period and for clarity to see His work in your life.

3   Scripture Meditation:

- Meditate on Genesis 17:1-13 and reflect on God's covenant with Abraham. Consider how this covenant relates to your personal promises from God.

4   Faith Affirmations:

- Create a list of affirmations based on God's promises to you. Repeat these affirmations daily to reinforce your faith and trust in His plan.

Quiz: Understanding the Chapter

1   Multiple Choice:

- What was Abraham's original name before God changed it?

    - a) Isaac
    - b) Jacob
    - c) Abram
    - d) Joseph

- Why did God make Abraham wait for His

promise?

- - a) To test Abraham's patience
- - b) To transform Abraham and Sarah into the people they needed to be
- - c) To delay the blessing
- - d) To give up on the promise

2   True or False:

- ○ Abraham and Sarah's wait for a child was short and easy.

  - - True
  - - False
- ○ Joseph's brothers sold him because they understood his dreams and wanted to help him.

  - - True
  - - False

3   Short Answer:

- ○ How did Joseph's ability to interpret dreams change his fate?
- ○ What significant lesson does the story of Moses in Midian teach us about waiting on God's timing?

Discussion Prompts

1   Group Discussion:

- ○ Share a story of a time when you waited for something significant and how it impacted your faith.

- ○ Discuss how waiting can be a period of growth and transformation rather than just a delay.

2 Role Play:

- ○ In pairs or small groups, role-play a scenario where someone is struggling with waiting for a promise and another person offers encouragement based on the stories of Abraham, Joseph, or Moses.

3 Application in Daily Life:

- ○ How can we apply the principles learned from Abraham, Joseph, and Moses to our daily lives and our own waiting periods?

Summary Reflection

- • Write a summary of how this chapter has impacted your understanding of waiting on God's promises. Include any new insights or changes in perspective you have gained.

This workbook is designed to help you deeply engage with the themes of patience, faith, and transformation during waiting periods. By reflecting on the experiences of biblical figures and relating them to your personal journey, you can find strength and encouragement in God's timing and promises.

Workbook Chapter Four:

The Assignment

Welcome to the workbook for Chapter 4, "The Assignment," from "The Answer: Not What I Imagined" by Joseph Brice. This chapter delves into the profound journey of Moses, focusing on his divine assignment to lead the Israelites out of bondage and his pivotal role in shaping religious history.

Chapter 4 explores the extraordinary moment when Moses encountered the burning bush, a divine manifestation that called him to a monumental task. Despite the awe-inspiring vision, Moses' initial response was marked by uncertainty and fear. He questioned God about His identity and the feasibility of his mission, illustrating a common human reaction to divine callings. This chapter examines how Moses grappled with his assignment, faced his fears, and ultimately embraced his role as a leader and prophet.

In this workbook, you will engage with activities designed to:

- **Reflect on Divine Assignments:** Understand the significance of responding to a higher calling, even when it seems daunting or unclear.
- **Examine Moses' Journey:** Analyze Moses' response to his divine assignment and how his story can inspire and guide you in addressing your own life challenges and responsibilities.
- **Identify Your Own Assignments:** Explore personal areas where you may be called to make a difference and reflect on how you can embrace and fulfill these roles.
- **Apply Biblical Lessons:** Learn from Moses' experiences to find courage and purpose in your own assignments,

recognizing that divine calls often come with challenges
but also with profound potential.

Through the exercises in this workbook, you will gain insights
into the nature of divine assignments and how to approach them
with faith and determination. You will be encouraged to see your
own challenges and responsibilities through the lens of Moses'
journey, finding inspiration and guidance for your own path.

Approach this workbook with an open mind and a willingness to
explore your unique calling. May the lessons from Moses' story
empower you to accept and excel in the assignments you face,
trusting in the divine purpose and guidance that accompanies
each call.

Reflective Questions

1   **Moses' Response:**

   - Why do you think Moses was the only one to
     respond to the burning bush?
   - How do you discern when you are being called by
     God for a specific assignment?

2   **Overcoming Fear:**

   - What fears did Moses face when called to return
     to Egypt?
   - How can we overcome similar fears when faced
     with daunting tasks or responsibilities?

3   **God's Assurance:**

   - How did God reassure Moses about his mission to

deliver the Israelites?

- ○ Can you recall a time when you felt reassured by God or your faith in a challenging situation?

4 Importance of the Assignment:

- ○ What significance does Moses' assignment hold in religious history?
- ○ How do you perceive the importance of your personal assignments or callings?

5 Endurance and Faith:

- ○ What challenges did Moses face during his journey with the Israelites?
- ○ How do you stay committed to your purpose despite facing obstacles and resistance?

Practice Exercises

1 Scripture Reflection:

- ○ Read and meditate on Exodus 3:1-14, focusing on Moses' encounter with the burning bush and his dialogue with God. Write down your reflections and how this passage speaks to your life.

2 Fear Inventory:

- ○ Make a list of your current fears or hesitations regarding any callings or tasks you feel drawn to. Next to each fear, write down a corresponding affirmation of faith or scripture that counters it.

3   Prayer for Guidance:

- Develop a prayer asking for clarity and courage to respond to your assignments. Pray daily for God's guidance and strength to fulfill your purpose.

4   Role Model Study:

- Choose a biblical or historical figure known for responding to a divine call. Study their life and note how they overcame challenges and stayed committed to their mission. Reflect on how their journey can inspire your own.

Quiz: Understanding the Chapter

1   Multiple Choice:

- What was Moses' initial reaction to the burning bush?

  - a) Ignored it
  - b) Ran away
  - c) Investigated it
  - d) Called for help

- What did God say His name was to Moses?

  - a) Yahweh
  - b) Jehovah
  - c) I AM THAT I AM
  - d) Elohim

2 True or False:

- Moses felt completely confident about returning to Egypt when God called him.

  - True
  - False

- The Israelites immediately accepted Moses' authority without any resistance.

  - True
  - False

3 Short Answer:

- Why was Moses hesitant to return to Egypt?
- What significance does the Passover Feast hold, and how did it originate?

Discussion Prompts

1 Group Discussion:

- Share a personal story of a time when you felt called to do something significant. How did you respond, and what was the outcome?
- Discuss the concept of "many are called, but few are chosen" and how it relates to personal dedication and response to God's call.

2 Role Play:

- In pairs or small groups, role-play a scenario where someone is struggling with a divine assignment, and another person offers support and encouragement based on Moses' story.

3   Application in Daily Life:

     ○   How can we apply the principles learned from Moses' story to our daily lives and our response to divine assignments?

Summary Reflection

- Write a summary of how this chapter has impacted your understanding of responding to divine assignments. Include any new insights or changes in perspective you have gained.

This workbook is designed to help you deeply engage with the themes of divine calling, fear, reassurance, and perseverance. By reflecting on the experiences of Moses and relating them to your personal journey, you can find strength and encouragement in fulfilling your assignments and purpose.

Workbook Chapter Five:

The Rejection

Welcome to the workbook for Chapter 5, The "Rejection from "The Answer: Not What I Imagined" by Joseph Brice. In this chapter, we delve into the critical importance of vigilance and self-awareness in our spiritual journey. "The Rejection" is a call to be mindful of the subtle influences and distractions that can lead us away from our true purpose and divine calling.

Jesus frequently admonished His followers to be watchful and alert. This chapter explores His teachings on the necessity of spiritual discernment and the dangers of complacency. By examining biblical examples and contemporary applications, we learn how to guard our hearts and minds against the pitfalls that threaten our spiritual growth.

The story of Judas Iscariot provides a stark illustration of the consequences of failing to heed Jesus' warnings. Despite being one of the twelve disciples, Judas allowed greed and disillusionment to corrupt his heart, leading to his betrayal of Jesus. This tragic tale serves as a powerful reminder that even those closest to the truth can falter if they do not remain vigilant.

In this workbook, you will find reflective questions, practical exercises, quizzes, and discussion prompts designed to help you internalize the lessons of Chapter 5. These activities will encourage you to assess your own spiritual state, identify areas where you need to be more watchful, and develop strategies to strengthen your faith and commitment.

Our goal is to equip you with the tools to stay alert and steadfast in your walk with God. By taking heed of Jesus' teachings and the examples set forth in the Bible, you can avoid the snares of the enemy and remain true to your divine calling.

Approach this chapter with an open mind and a willing spirit, ready to learn and grow. As you engage with the content, may you develop a heightened sense of spiritual awareness and a deeper commitment to living a life that honors God. Through vigilance and faithfulness, you can navigate the challenges of this world and stay on the path to your ultimate purpose.

This chapter takes us into a profound exploration of rejection and its role in the journey of faith. It draws on the experiences of Jesus in His hometown of Nazareth and contrasts this with His acceptance and impact in Capernaum.

Chapter 5 highlights the reality that rejection is often an integral part of fulfilling one's divine calling. Despite Jesus' miraculous works and authoritative teachings, He faced intense rejection from those who could not see beyond their preconceived notions. This chapter underscores how rejection can be a painful but pivotal aspect of spiritual growth and effectiveness.

In this workbook, you will engage with exercises and reflections that will help you:

- **Explore the Impact of Rejection:** Understand how rejection can influence your spiritual journey and how to respond constructively.
- **Examine Jesus' Example:** Reflect on how Jesus handled rejection and what His response teaches us about perseverance and faith.
- **Identify Personal Rejections:** Recognize and process areas in your life where you may be experiencing rejection, and discover ways to move forward.
- **Apply Lessons to Your Life:** Learn strategies for dealing with rejection and finding new opportunities for ministry and growth.

* * *

Through the activities in this workbook, you will be equipped to navigate the challenges of rejection with grace and resilience. You will gain insights into how rejection can serve as a catalyst for deeper faith and greater alignment with God's purposes.

Approach this workbook with an open heart, ready to confront and understand the role of rejection in your spiritual journey. As you engage with these materials, may you find encouragement and strength to embrace your calling, despite the challenges that come your way.

Reflective Questions

1   Expectations vs. Reality:

- Why did the people of Nazareth reject Jesus despite his fulfillment of Messianic criteria?
- How do you deal with unmet expectations from those around you, especially when you are doing something important?

2   Rejection and Ministry:

- How does Jesus' experience in Nazareth illustrate the challenges of ministering in one's hometown?
- Reflect on a time when you felt rejected or unappreciated by those close to you. How did you handle it?

3   Faith and Miracles:

- ○ Why was Jesus able to perform miracles in Capernaum but not in Nazareth?
- ○ How does faith play a role in experiencing and receiving God's works in your life?

4 Perception and Acceptance:

- ○ How did the negative perceptions of Jesus and Mary affect his ministry in Nazareth?
- ○ How can you overcome negative perceptions or judgments from others in pursuing your purpose?

5 Significance of Sacrifice:

- ○ What is the importance of Jesus' crucifixion and resurrection in Christian faith?
- ○ How can you embody the principles of sacrifice and redemption in your daily life?

Practice Exercises

1 Scripture Reflection:

- ○ Read and meditate on Luke 4:14-32. Write down your reflections on Jesus' rejection in Nazareth and how this passage speaks to your life.

2 Faith Inventory:

- ○ List areas in your life where you need to increase your faith. Next to each area, write a corresponding scripture that encourages faith and belief.

3 Prayer for Strength:

- o Develop a prayer asking for strength and resilience in the face of rejection and challenges. Pray daily for God's guidance and support.

4 Role Model Study:

- o Choose a biblical or historical figure known for dealing with rejection or challenges. Study their life and note how they overcame obstacles and stayed committed to their mission. Reflect on how their journey can inspire your own.

Quiz: Understanding the Chapter

1 Multiple Choice:

- o Why did the people of Nazareth reject Jesus?
  - ▪ a) They didn't understand his teachings
  - ▪ b) They wanted a king like David or Solomon
  - ▪ c) They were jealous of his abilities
  - ▪ d) They didn't know who he was
- o What was Jesus' response to the rejection in Nazareth?
  - ▪ a) He argued with them
  - ▪ b) He performed miracles to prove himself
  - ▪ c) He left Nazareth and went to Capernaum
  - ▪ d) He cursed them

2   True or False:

- Jesus performed many miracles in Nazareth.

    - True
    - False
- The people of Capernaum believed in Jesus and respected his authority.

    - True
    - False

3   Short Answer:

- How did Jesus use the stories of Elijah and Elisha to address the people of Nazareth?
- What is the significance of the brazen serpent in the context of Jesus' sacrifice?

Discussion Prompts

1   Group Discussion:

- Share a personal story of a time when you felt rejected. How did you cope, and what did you learn from the experience?
- Discuss the concept of finding vindication and justice through Christ's redemption and how it applies to personal experiences of injustice.

2   Role Play:

o   In pairs or small groups, role-play a scenario where someone faces rejection while trying to fulfill their calling. Practice offering support and encouragement based on Jesus' story.

3   Application in Daily Life:

o   How can we apply the principles learned from Jesus' experience of rejection to our daily lives and our response to challenges and setbacks?

Summary Reflection

•   Write a summary of how this chapter has impacted your understanding of dealing with rejection and remaining faithful to your mission. Include any new insights or changes in perspective you have gained.

This workbook is designed to help you deeply engage with the themes of rejection, faith, resilience, and redemption. By reflecting on the experiences of Jesus and relating them to your personal journey, you can find strength and encouragement in fulfilling your purpose and mission.

Workbook Chapter Six:

Faith To Obey

Welcome to the workbook for Chapter 6, "Faith to Obey," from "The Answer: Not What I Imagined" by Joseph Brice. This chapter explores the profound connection between faith and obedience, highlighting the spiritual battle between our divine calling and the worldly influences that seek to derail us. Through the lens of biblical narratives and personal reflection, we uncover the significance of faith in following God's commands and fulfilling our purpose.

The story of Simon Peter serves as a powerful illustration of this theme. Jesus addressed Simon by his original name to remind him of his human frailties, yet called him Peter to affirm his divine potential. This duality reflects the struggle we all face between our fleshly nature and our spiritual calling. Jesus' prayer for Simon's faith to remain steadfast despite the enemy's attempts to sift him as wheat resonates deeply, reminding us that our faith is both a shield and a pathway to transformation.

In this workbook, you will engage with reflective questions, practice exercises, quizzes, and discussion prompts designed to deepen your understanding of the interplay between faith and obedience. You will be encouraged to examine your own life, identify the areas where faith needs to be strengthened, and commit to following God's will with unwavering trust.

Our aim is to help you recognize the power of faith in overcoming obstacles and staying true to your divine purpose. By reflecting on the lessons from Simon Peter's journey and Jesus' teachings, you can find the courage to obey God's commands, even when faced with adversity.

We invite you to approach this chapter with an open heart, ready to explore the depths of your faith and discover the strength that comes from complete surrender to God. Through this journey, may you find the inspiration to obey God with confidence, knowing that His plans for you are far greater than you can imagine.

Reflective Questions

1 Faith and Obedience:

- Why does it take faith to obey God, especially in challenging circumstances?
- Can you recall a time when obeying God required significant faith? How did you respond, and what was the outcome?

2 Identity and Nature:

- What is the significance of Jesus addressing Simon by his original name rather than Peter?
- How does understanding your spiritual identity versus your fleshly nature impact your faith and actions?

3 Generational Curses:

- How does Jesus' work on the cross address the concept of generational curses?
- Reflect on any perceived generational issues in your family. How can faith in Jesus help you

overcome these?

4   Purpose and Calling:

- How does discovering and fulfilling your purpose align with bringing glory to God?
- What steps can you take to identify your true calling and align your actions with it?

5   Spiritual Warfare:

- How does the enemy target our faith, and why is it crucial to protect it?
- Share an experience where your faith was tested. How did you hold on to your faith during that time?

Practice Exercises

1   Scripture Reflection:

- Read and meditate on Luke 22:31. Write down your reflections on Jesus' warning to Simon and how it applies to your life.

2   Faith Inventory:

- Identify areas in your life where your faith is being challenged. Next to each area, write a corresponding scripture that encourages faith and resilience.

3   Purpose Discovery:

- Spend time in prayer and reflection to identify your passions, talents, and strengths. Write down practical ways you can use these to serve others and fulfill your divine purpose.

4   Affirmation of Identity:

- Write affirmations based on your spiritual identity in Christ. Repeat these affirmations daily to reinforce your true nature and calling.

Quiz: Understanding the Chapter

1   Multiple Choice:

- Why did Jesus address Simon by his original name?

  - a) To remind him of his past
  - b) To highlight his fleshly nature
  - c) To show affection
  - d) To confuse him

- What is the enemy's primary target according to this chapter?

  - a) Your health
  - b) Your family
  - c) Your faith
  - d) Your wealth

2   True or False:

- Jesus came to remove generational curses from their source.

    - True
    - False
- Fulfilling your divine purpose will always be easy and without opposition.

    - True
    - False

3   Short Answer:

- How does understanding your purpose help you resist the enemy's attacks?
- Explain the significance of faith in overcoming challenges and fulfilling your divine mission.

Discussion Prompts

1   Group Discussion:

- Share a personal story of a time when your faith was challenged. How did you overcome it, and what did you learn from the experience?
- Discuss the importance of understanding our true identity in Christ and how it influences our actions and decisions.

2   Role Play:

- In pairs or small groups, role-play a scenario where someone faces a challenge to their faith. Practice offering support and encouragement based on the principles from this chapter.

3   Application in Daily Life:

- o   How can we apply the principles learned from this chapter to our daily lives and our response to challenges and setbacks?

Summary Reflection

- •   Write a summary of how this chapter has impacted your understanding of faith, obedience, and spiritual warfare. Include any new insights or changes in perspective you have gained.

This workbook is designed to help you deeply engage with the themes of faith, obedience, spiritual identity, and purpose. By reflecting on these concepts and relating them to your personal journey, you can find strength and encouragement in fulfilling your divine mission and resisting the enemy's attacks.

Workbook Chapter Seven:

The Answer

Welcome to the workbook for Chapter 7, "The Answer," from "The Answer: Not What I Imagined" by Joseph Brice. This chapter delves into the profound lessons of faith, perseverance, and the divine guidance that shapes our journey. Through the story of David's trials and triumphs, we uncover the essence of compassion and the importance of recognizing Jesus as the ultimate answer to our challenges and questions.

David's experiences, from receiving a prophecy of kingship to facing relentless adversity, mirror the struggles we encounter in our own lives. His unwavering faith and commitment to seeking God's guidance offer us a powerful model for navigating our paths. The chapter also highlights the transformative power of compassion, as seen in David's interaction with the Egyptian, and the critical role of forgiveness in freeing ourselves from the burdens of past hurts.

In this workbook, you will find reflective questions, practice exercises, quizzes, and discussion prompts designed to deepen your understanding of these themes. As you engage with the material, you will be encouraged to reflect on your own experiences, seek divine guidance, and embody the love and forgiveness of Jesus in your daily interactions.

Our goal is to help you uncover the answers to your life's challenges through a closer relationship with God. By exploring the lessons from David's journey and Jesus' ultimate sacrifice, you can find strength, hope, and the assurance that Jesus is indeed The Answer to all your needs.

We invite you to embark on this journey with an open heart and mind, ready to discover the profound truths that will guide you towards a more fulfilling and purposeful life.

Reflective Questions

1   David's Adversity:

- How did David's commitment to the prophecy help him navigate his challenges?
- Reflect on a time when you faced significant adversity. How did your faith help you through it?

2   Divine Guidance:

- What can we learn from David's response to seeking guidance from God during his trials?
- When faced with uncertainty, how do you seek and recognize guidance from God?

3   Compassion in Action:

- David showed compassion to a stranger who ultimately provided crucial information. How can compassion and kindness in unexpected situations lead to unexpected answers?
- Share an instance when helping someone unexpectedly led to a positive outcome for you.

4   Jesus as The Answer:

- How does understanding Jesus as the ultimate answer change your perspective on handling life's problems?
- In what ways can you embody the love and forgiveness of Jesus in your daily interactions?

5 Forgiveness and Liberation:

- How does forgiving those who have wronged you liberate you from pain and resentment?
- Describe a situation where forgiving someone brought you peace and healing.

Practice Exercises

1 Scripture Reflection:

- Read and meditate on Isaiah 53:1-10. Write down your reflections on how this prophecy relates to Jesus being the answer to humanity's needs.

2 Compassion Journal:

- Keep a journal for a week, noting instances where you showed compassion or kindness. Reflect on how these actions impacted you and others.

3 Forgiveness Exercise:

- Write a letter to someone you need to forgive. You don't have to send it, but express your feelings and release any lingering resentment or pain.

4   Prayer and Guidance:

- Spend time in prayer, asking God for guidance in a current challenge. Write down any thoughts, scriptures, or insights you receive.

Quiz: Understanding the Chapter

1   Multiple Choice:

- Why did David's men turn on him after the attack on Ziklag?

  - a) They were angry and frustrated
  - b) They were ordered by King Saul
  - c) They found new leaders
  - d) They wanted to return to Israel

- What was the young Egyptian's role in David's recovery of his family and possessions?

  - a) He provided information on the location of the Amalekites
  - b) He fought alongside David
  - c) He healed David's wounds
  - d) He betrayed David

2   True or False:

- Jesus is referred to as the ultimate answer to all of humanity's questions and problems.

  - True
  - False

- ○ David was financially stable after recovering everything from the Amalekites.

    - ▪ True
    - ▪ False

3   Short Answer:

- ○ How does Jesus' experience of rejection and suffering demonstrate his role as The Answer for humanity?
- ○ Why is it important to forgive those who have wronged us, according to the chapter?

Discussion Prompts

1   Group Discussion:

- ○ Share a time when you felt like David, facing overwhelming adversity. How did you find your way through it, and what role did your faith play?
- ○ Discuss the importance of being compassionate and kind to strangers, as demonstrated by David's interaction with the Egyptian.

2   Role Play:

- ○ In pairs or small groups, role-play a scenario where someone is struggling with unforgiveness. Practice offering support and encouragement based on the principles from this chapter.

3   Application in Daily Life:

- How can you apply the lesson of Jesus being the ultimate answer to your current challenges?
- Reflect on ways to embody Jesus' love and forgiveness in your daily life and interactions.

Summary Reflection

- Write a summary of how this chapter has impacted your understanding of compassion, forgiveness, and recognizing Jesus as the ultimate answer. Include any new insights or changes in perspective you have gained.

This workbook is designed to help you deeply engage with the themes of adversity, compassion, forgiveness, and recognizing Jesus as The Answer. By reflecting on these concepts and relating them to your personal journey, you can find strength and encouragement in embodying these principles in your daily life.

Dear Reader,

As you come to the end of this workbook, we hope you have found clarity, inspiration, and a deeper understanding of the journey towards discovering the answers you seek. "The Answer" is more than just a workbook; it's a guide to spiritual and personal growth, anchored in the timeless truths of faith and the transformative power of God's love.

Prayer of Salvation

Scripture says, "Whoever calls upon the name of the Lord will be saved." If you would like to know Christ, you can receive the free gift of salvation through Jesus Christ by praying for salvation. Please say this prayer out loud:

"Oh merciful Lord Jesus, I humble myself before you and sincerely apologize for my transgressions. I acknowledge that I have strayed from your ways and ask for your forgiveness. Please purify me of my sins and make me clean. I firmly believe that you are the Son of God, who sacrificed your life on the cross out of love for humanity to redeem us all. On the third day, you rose again, triumphant over death and sin, and bestowed the gift of eternal life upon us. With all my heart, I profess that you are my Savior and Lord, and I pledge to follow you throughout my life. Amen."

Prayer for the New Beginner

Dear Heavenly Father,

As a new believer, I humbly come before you, seeking your guidance and grace on this faith journey. I am grateful for your Word that brings hope, strength, and assurance of your love for me. As I delve into the Scriptures, I pray that they become a lamp to my feet and a light to my path.

Please help me grow in my relationship with you and trust your plans for my life. May I find comfort in your presence, and may my life testify to your love for those around me.

I fervently pray in the name of our Lord and Savior, Jesus Christ. Amen.

If you have recently embarked on this new chapter of faith, we rejoice with you and congratulate you on this significant step. We eagerly await hearing from you about your decision, praying with you, and providing you with the necessary materials and guidance as you begin your journey.

Prayer 1

Dear Father,

We are grateful that you sent us the answer in the form of your Son, Jesus. Dear Lord, we humbly ask for your divine wisdom and discernment to recognize the things that are meant to come from you. Please help us see your answers to our prayers, no matter what form they take. We acknowledge our past mistakes of rejecting and mistreating your blessings and seek your forgiveness. May we never again miss an opportunity to receive your grace and mercy. Thank you for your unwavering love and guidance. Amen.

Please grant us another chance to receive the answer that you've sent us. Help us to see what You see and guide us towards a path of righteousness in Jesus's name.

Prayer 2

As a devout Christian, I believe that the power of Jesus Christ is my ultimate salvation. Trusting in God is more than just a statement of faith; it's a testament to my unwavering commitment to following Jesus as my Lord and Savior. Through prayer, I express my gratitude, confess my sins, and seek forgiveness and guidance. It's an intimate worship act that reflects my deep relationship with God and my unwavering desire to live according to his teachings. I pray that my faith in Jesus never wavers and that I may always walk in his light.

Contact Us

We encourage you to reach out to us at Kingdom Rights if you have any questions, need further guidance, or simply want to share your journey with us. We are here to support you and help you grow in your faith.

Website: kingdomrights2.org
Email: info@kingdomrights2.org

May God bless you abundantly as you continue to seek His will and walk in His ways. Always remember, you are never alone on this journey—God's love, wisdom, and grace are with you every step of the way.

With heartfelt blessings,

Joseph Brice